T0164984

"THE Spirit OF THE Horse"

AND OTHER WORKS

PHIL RAY JACK

abbott press®

A DIVISION OF WRITER'S DIGEST

Abbott Press books may be ordered through booksellers or by contacting:

Abbott Press
1663 Liberty Drive
Bloomington, IN 47403
www.abbottpress.com
Phone: 1-866-697-5310

Because of the dynamic nature of the Internet, any web addresses or
links contained in this book may have changed since publication and
may no longer be valid. The views expressed in this work are solely those
of the author and do not necessarily reflect the views of the publisher,
and the publisher hereby disclaims any responsibility for them.

Any people depicted in stock imagery provided by Thinkstock are models,
and such images are being used for illustrative purposes only.

Certain stock imagery © Thinkstock.

ISBN: 978-1-4582-0819-4 (sc)
ISBN: 978-1-4582-0817-0 (e)

Library of Congress Control Number: 2013902526

Printed in the United States of America

Abbott Press rev. date: 2/18/2013

Dedication

This book is dedicated to my best friend, Diane. She stood by me through tough times, has been and continues to be a light for me in my darkness, and has helped me find my authentic self. In doing so, she helped me understand what it really means to be a true friend. For that, I will always be grateful.

"It's the possibility of having a dream come true that makes life interesting."
—Paulo Coelho, *The Alchemist*

Table of Contents

List of Illustrations

Introduction

When I began this project, my intent was to simply gather some of my poems and publish them as a collection, but as I did so, I realized that there was a theme – that these poems were actually signposts along the path of my life. I realized that most readers would not notice, and those who did would do so because they have shared in my journey. I struggled with my desire to explain how each poem falls into place and the realization that, for most people, it won't matter.

I have been working on a couple of novels that will be following this book, but it seemed right to start with this one. Like most writers, I am motivated by a lot of different things. Sometimes I'm promoting a cause I believe in. Sometimes I want people to better understand the complexities of the world we live in. I have stories to tell, and by telling them, I'm hoping to teach.

But I write poetry for myself. Sometimes I have thoughts and feelings trapped inside that have no other way of getting out. I don't know why writing poetry works for me – I only know that it does. When I was younger, I would hide my poems so that no one else would know what was going on in my head and in my heart. Eventually, I would share a poem with a friend or a family member. Of course, they would praise me and tell me how wonderful my poems are – after all, that's why we share things like this with family and friends. We seek affirmation. We want to be told that what we think and feel matters.

It took a long time for me to share my poetry with "the public." I began by sharing a couple of my poems in Creative Writing classes. While most students tend to live by the principle of "If I'm nice to you, maybe you'll be nice to me," there are always those who freely offer criticism – perhaps living by the principle of "If I can find enough wrong with your work, I can feel better about my own." To my surprise, I escaped relatively unscathed. In fact, a couple of my poems found their way into *Genesis*, Adams State College's art and literature magazine.

Eventually I entered some contests, and while the only time I won first prize was for a limerick that the school refused to publish (I followed the traditional form for limerick's – it was a little "colorful."), my work usually found its way to the middle. Considering some of the poets whose works scored more highly than mine, I'm okay with that.

After all, I wrote them for me, so it was enough to have a few people enjoy them without the pressure of having to because of their friendship or family ties with me.

So, when I realized that there was a theme, it really was a struggle to decide whether I wanted to point that out – perhaps even highlight it – or if I wanted to let the readers discover it on their own.

I chose a compromise. I've already told you that these poems mark significant points in my journey to discover my authentic self. (Yes, I do realize that is a "buzz word," and like most buzz words, its significance may be weakened by its popularity, but there is nothing "weak" about discovering who you truly are and learning how to nourish that true self, so I'm going to continue using it.) You may also notice that, even when I was on my path alone, I looked for help along the way. I found that help when I met and grew to know my best friend – and I realized I was writing about her even before I met her.

So that's an important part of it. As you read through these poems, though, you may find yourself wondering "What lesson or significant event is this poem about?" Just keep reading and let the pieces fall into place.

I've also included a few columns. I've written *It Seems to Me* for the *Valley Courier* in Alamosa, Colorado, and the *Cibola County Beacon* in Grants, New Mexico. These columns help connect the theme of this book.

About horses: My journey became clear when I climbed into the saddle, and to this day, I find comfort, healing and clarity when I am on the back of a horse. Those who love horses as I do will feel the presence of their spirit throughout this book.

I hope you enjoy it. Even more, I hope that something within it will speak to you. After all, as different as we all are, we really are alike.

It Seems to Me:
Coming Home

After moving away more than twenty years ago, I returned to the San Luis Valley last June. While I enjoyed most of the places I've lived, it feels great to be back home again.

I left to pursue a career teaching in college, and for more that seventeen years, I struggled to survive as a "professional part-time instructor" while trying to land a full-time position. A lot of people are surprised when they hear that approximately eighty percent of college classes are taught by adjunct, or part-time, instructors, and that there is a lot of competition of full-time positions.

I eventually realized that if you don't like the way things are, you can either work to change them or remain miserable until someone else does something, and I became involved in our faculty union. A couple of years later, I became the first part-time instructor in the history of the State of Washington to be elected president of a faculty union local.

Finally, after more than seventeen years of a career that spanned three states and included teaching for seven institutions of higher learning, I was hired as a full-time instructor. I felt this was the culmination of my hopes and dreams.

The tenure process is much more grueling than most

people realize. While each state and institution has its own set of guidelines, they all strive to assure that those who are granted tenure will maintain high standards of learning. In my case, I worked with a committee comprised of three faculty members (one from our division, one selected by the union, and one that I chose), an administrator, and a student. For three years, they observed my classes, conducted student evaluations, and offered constructive criticism and guidance.

Unfortunately, in spite of the fact that my committee unanimously recommended that I be granted tenure, the Board of Trustees rejected my application and gave me an additional year to work on an improvement plan. The recommendation of a committee comprised of professional educators who had worked closely with me for three years (not including the ten years I had worked there as a part-time instructor and the president of the faculty union) was rejected based on anonymous student responses to two questions on student evaluations in two of my classes.

And then, last January, I almost lost both of my parents and flew back so that I could spend what I thought were their last days with them. The timing couldn't have been worse. I left at the same time my tenure committee was making their final recommendation, but my family came first.

Fortunately, my parents are stubborn enough to pull through, and are doing fine, but a few weeks after I returned to Seattle, I was given the choice between resigning or having my tenure application rejected.

My best friend, Diane, saw my struggles and took me to a ranch where she was taking riding lessons.

On that first day, I simply helped lead the horses from

their pastures to their stables and watched Diane as she rode, but being near the horses fed a part of my soul that I had ignored for too long. I went back to the ranch a week later and paid for a private lesson.

As soon as I sat in the saddle, everything became clear to me. It had been more than twenty years since I had been on a horse, and I had forgotten how much I love being in the saddle.

I realized that I needed to be in a place where I could have a horse underneath me and the Rockies at my back, and I decided it was time for me to return to my roots and to my real, authentic self.

For years, I had boasted that my friends and family get frustrated on my birthdays and Christmas because they don't have any idea what to get me. I believed that it was because my life was complete and that I had everything I wanted, but when I sat in that saddle, I realized that I had become so caught up in providing service to others -- both as a teacher and a leader in the union -- that I had lost sight of who I am. I really didn't even know what I wanted out of life -- how could anyone else?

It was hard to leave Seattle. I had made a lot of friends, and all three of my daughters, as well as my two granddaughters, live in Washington State. At that time, I believed it would mean ending my career as a teacher, and it meant walking away from a relationship that had become very important to me. At least, that's how I felt at the time.

In spite of all these things, I knew it was a move I had to make. I didn't feel like I was running away from anything, rather I felt like I was moving toward my future.

But once I made the decision, things seemed to fall into place for me. The huge issues and problems I had been dealing with didn't disappear, but I realized that they weren't as overwhelming as they had seemed. I worked to the end of my contract and used the time to gain a better understanding of who I am and what I want to accomplish in my life.

My sister helped me find the cabin in South Fork, Colorado, so that I had a place to live when I got here. I only brought the possessions I could get into my van, and I started building my new life from scratch.

When I reached my new home, I started getting ready for a horse. I began looking for a place to keep him. I heard that feed is pretty scarce this year, so I bought enough hay and oats to feed two horses for a year. A few people felt it was strange that I bought feed and had found a pasture when I didn't even own a horse! Still, I didn't want to own a horse and not have anything to feed it or a place to keep it.

Now, I own two horses, Wink and Colorado Rose, and I spend as much time in the saddle as I possibly can.

I begin my day sitting next to the river and enjoying the peaceful sounds of the morning. I'm close to family and get to see my parents often. I'm currently teaching a class at Adams State, and in a few months, I will be publishing a collection of my poems and reflections followed by a novel that I'm working on.

I've re-discovered myself, and I'm getting to know myself better every day.

It feels good to be home again.

(**Note:** Since this column was originally published, I've gotten a third horse – Midnight Wind. Life is good.)

*"As soon as I sat in the saddle, everything
became clear to me ..."*

Soar High

Soar high,
My well-loved friend,
And fly without fear.
If you should ever need me,
Just call,
And I'll be near.

Remember:

The skies were not made
For those afraid to fly,
Nor dreams,
For those afraid to live,
So unfold your wings,
Dream your dreams,
And give life
All you have to give.

It Seems to Me:
Attitude Plus Effort

Recently I was reminded of a story I heard on one of the episodes of the *West Wing* television series. An old man and a young man are sitting on a porch when a passing traveler asks. "I'm moving to the next town, and I was wondering if you could tell me what it's like."

"What was the last town you lived in like?" the old man asks.

"It was great! I really hated to leave. People were friendly, and I made a lot of good friends there."

"That's what the next town is like," answered the old man, and the traveler smiled and continued on his journey.

After awhile, another traveler stopped and said, "Excuse me, but I'm moving to the next town. Could you tell me what it's like?"

Once again, the old man asked, "What was the last town you lived in like?"

"It was terrible," the traveler answered. "I couldn't trust anyone. Everyone was out to get ahead, and they'd stab you in the back to get there. I hated it, and I was glad to leave."

"I'm afraid that it's the same in the next town," the old man said.

After the second traveler left, the young man pointed out,

"You gave completely different answers to each traveler, yet they are both going to the same town. Which was the true answer?"

"Both answers were true," said the old man. "Our lives are determined more by our attitudes than circumstances. Each traveler will find what they expect in the next town."

Of course, that is oversimplifying things. In *Winning Through Intimidation*, Robert J. Ringer points out that having a positive attitude is not enough. We not only have to believe that we will succeed, but we also have to work to make positive things happen. Sometimes we also have to recognize that, no matter what we do, we can't control the actions and choices made by others. We may be able to influence them (but often we aren't even able to accomplish that), but we can't control them.

And sometimes circumstances make it difficult to maintain a positive attitude. As we go through life, we all experience disappointment and loss.

But having a positive attitude can help us get through the hard times and help us to accomplish goals. If we don't believe we can make a difference or change the circumstances of our life, we won't try. Of course, having a positive attitude won't accomplish anything unless we back it up with action.

Another Day

It used to be
That seconds ticked softly
While hands slowly
Circled clocks' faces.

Now
Bright red numbers
Flash warnings
That time is rushing by.

That second's gone ...
Another ... another ...
Hours lost –
Days rush by.
"What have I done?"

Three hundred emails
Answered yesterday!
Two meetings!
Decisions made!
Tasks Completed!
Life set aside.

The sun set unnoticed.
Silvery raindrops
Fell from fresh leaves.
All unseen.

A little girl smiled
And reached for me –
"Poppa! Poppa!"
I picked her up,
Felt her small arms squeeze
As she says,
"Hugs make me Happy!"

"A little girl smiled and reached for me."

Storm on the Horizon

Lightening dances across the horizon
Racing from dark clouds blanketing rocky peaks
To snow-capped Sandia.
Overhead, stars sparkle just beyond our reach
Beckoning for attention.
Below, city lights crowd the mesa on which we stand,
Making Albuquerque seem so alive we could watch it grow.
On the mesa,
We sit,
Breathing in life,
Feeling it tickle our souls.
Cary picks at guitar strings
And sings a song he wrote.
His music tells of a love lived, love lost,
And the pain felt deep inside.
He sees the storm clouds,
Still feels the rain.
The storm has passed,
And another might follow,
But--right now--
I see the stars,
And I can't keep from reaching for them.

Soon, the early morning sun
Pushes the clouds away.
There's life in the sunshine,
There's also life in the rain.
And, sometimes it's easy to see love,
But, there's also love in the pain,
Denying love means living empty.
I can't turn away from the stars
Just because I've felt the rain.

"Lightening dances across the horizon ..."

Deserted Shack

Blind windows miss the blue sky,
Don't see tender blossoms growing
Between splintered planks.
Don't feel the sun glow
On its worn-out face.

Silent doorway is empty
Except for blades of grass
That can't avoid
Being pushed across the threshold
By uncaring breezes.

Once-strong walls shudder
For lack of purpose.
The lives they sheltered
No longer visit,
No longer care.

"Blind windows miss the blue sky …"

The Marker

A dusty, white wooden cross
　　　marks where you rest.
I read the dates, and my mind
　　　races to a place
　　　without roads, without fields,
　　　only prairie.
　　　A place where buffalo belong,
　　　their huge frames covered
　　　with shaggy, dark fur,
　　　near-black manes hiding their humps.
　　　It is a time when they belonged
　　　more than we,
　　　when The People lived with the land
　　　before you conquered the land.

I wonder:
　　　Were there days when
You stood, clenching
　　　dirt-covered, scarred fists,
　　　with the moisture from your eyes
　　　as out-of-place in this arid land
　　　as you?

Did you wonder why,
    no matter what you did,
no matter how hard you tried,
    no matter how hard you worked,
You just couldn't get by?

And were there days when
    the sun felt warm, not hot,
    on your face, and you
    stopped to wipe the sweat from
    your brow,
And it just felt good to live?

How many times did you feel
    your lover's touch as her
    gentle hand brushed your cheek
    and her soft flesh became yours.

Mom says you died in a train robbery,
    but, as I look at the white, dusty splinters
    of the wooden cross, I wonder
How you lived.

    Were you just like me?

"A place where buffalo belong, their huge frames covered with shaggy, dark fur ..."

Son's Pride

We sit
Side-by-side
In kicked-back recliners,
His old, patched, broken-in,
Mine merely scuffed.

Silence.
I stare at new novel,
Wonder what he's thinking.
Notice heavy, black work-boots
Still worn, have holes.

Want to discuss Emerson,
Realize Emerson would mean no more
Than others who have tried to guide his life,
Or judge it.

He's happy with himself.
So am I.
Push myself out of chair,
Grab coat.
"See ya later, Dad."
"Sure, Son."

No other title worn with more pride.

It Seems to Me:
Leon Jack, This One's for You

D ad says he's glad I haven't mentioned his name in my column because he wants to avoid "guilt by association," but the example he has set for us is worth sharing. As my best friend put it, "People deserve to hear about amazing people and know there is a different way to face life."

I can't think of a better way to describe him. Dad is truly an amazing man who has found a different way to face life. He has met life's challenges head on and with a sense of humor. Mom often tells me, "I don't know how he does it, but he doesn't let anything keep him down, and he just keeps on going."

I've learned a lot from Dad. He has always taught more by example than with words, and one of the first things I learned from him was to never let others set the standard for me to live by. He taught me to choose the path that is most fulfilling rather than the one that pays the most. While others sought material things, Dad always valued a different type of treasure.

Too many times, when we are forced to choose between our families and our careers, we will make the practical choice of our careers. Often we tell ourselves this is a temporary decision, but when we constantly choose our careers first, our priorities are set.

Dad has worn a multitude of labels – bus driver, math

teacher, carpenter, electrician, television repairman and turquoise dealer – but the ones he took most seriously were "father" and "husband."

I suppose I could complain about being poor when I was growing up – and to be honest, I often have – but I never doubted that Dad loved us more than any job that he ever held. While others sought material things, he gave us a treasure that is much more valuable – his time. And while we may not have had the nicest clothes or the newest toys, we never went hungry and we had the things that really mattered. We learned to value the thought behind gifts more than the price tags. Even more importantly, I have memories of Dad always being around when I needed him, and I never doubted his love.

Dad taught me to believe in myself. When I first announced that I wanted to be a writer, most people cautioned me that I would probably never be able to make a living writing. Dad brought an application to Rod Serling's Famous Writers School and helped me fill it out. I knew that he believed in me and would stand beside me no matter what course I chose for my life – and he always has. He has often told me, "All of the money in the world will never substitute for feeling good about yourself."

I also appreciate the lessons I've learned from watching how Dad treats Mom. "Your Mom could have had any man she wanted, and sometimes I wonder why she picked me," he once said. "It always makes me want to be a better man so that I can deserve her."

I'm not saying they were always the perfect couple, but if they ever fought, it wasn't in front of us. I do remember Mom telling him once, "Why don't you ever tease me, Leon? You tease everyone else."

"Because you're my wife, and I always want to treat you with respect," Dad answered.

Mom insisted that she already knew he respected her and said she wanted to know that he liked her, too. I don't think Dad's quit teasing her since, and it always makes her smile.

Last January, we were convinced that we were going to lose them both, and were trying to prepare ourselves. Dad had been sick for several months and was steadily getting worse. He was in Intensive Care in Alamosa. On her way to see him, Mom had fallen and suffered serious injuries. She was in the hospital in La Jara.

We walked into Dad's room on the day of their 60th Anniversary, and he could barely move his head. It took all of the strength he could gather to whisper, "Where's your mom?" We explained that she had fallen and was in another hospital.

That was all it took. Mom needed him, and Dad wasn't going to let anything keep him from her. In a matter of days, Dad was on his feet and his health had improved enough for him to be transferred to the same Long-Term Care facility that Mom was in. Now they are both home and doing well.

So, thank you Dad for teaching me about what really matters in life.

It Seems to Me:
This One's for You, Mom

When I think of strong, independent women I admire, the first one who comes to mind is my mother, Lena Loy Jack. When I think of the things she has accomplished in her life, especially considering what she has had to overcome, I am amazed.

A few weeks ago, I received a voicemail from Mom saying that she was on her way from Manassa to Alamosa for her doctor's appointment, and that her van had overheated. I tried to return her call, but she didn't answer so I called my brother-in-law and started driving to find her.

In my mind, I saw my poor mother stuck on the side of the road waiting for me to rescue her. In reality, she had gotten a a ride and had made it to her doctor's appointment on time. I shouldn't have been surprised – Mom always finds a way to do things herself. Okay, she did get some help from the family friend who noticed the van stopped on the side of the road, but the point is, she didn't wait for me to rescue her.

When she was little, Mom was diagnosed with a slight heart murmur, so she grew up being told what she couldn't do. Then she began proving to people that they were wrong by doing it. For a variety of reasons, she didn't complete high school. That didn't stop her from finding a career that she enjoyed, though.

During the Korean War, Mom moved from the Valley while Dad served as a transport driver at a training base. She got a job as a nurse's aide, and since she loved children, worked her way into the maternity ward of a hospital. She knew what she wanted to do, and then found a way to do it.

Like most independent women, Mom didn't really appreciate her own inner strength. She accomplished amazing things, and would then be surprised to learn that people were impressed by what she had done. While I was going to college, I asked her why she had never gotten her GED and talked her into taking the test. She passed, got her diploma, and started signing up for college classes.

After a few years, her college counselors started telling her what classes she needed to take so that she could get her degree, and she quit going. "I just wanted to learn," she explained. "I didn't want to get a degree!"

Mom was afraid to fly until, when I was twenty-one, we almost lost her. She was rushed to Denver on the Flight for Life helicopter, where she was told that her chances for survival were slim. She not only stubbornly held on, but decided that if she could survive that flight, she could handle others and began flying out to see friends and relatives in other states.

There are numerous other stories I could tell about how Mom has overcome obstacles to accomplish her goals, but there is another powerful lesson that I've learned from her. She has not only shown me how to love and appreciate strong, independent women – she has taught me the value of partnership in relationships.

I remember Dad saying many times, "When I got married, I let my wife know who wears the pants in our family – and they look pretty good on her, too!"

I wouldn't go so far as to say that Mom was the head of our family, but I wouldn't say that about Dad, either. They have always been true partners, sharing in responsibility and working together through whatever trials they faced.

On occasion, when I'm in a discussion with someone about the importance of the man being the head of the household, I'll always ask, "Why?"

"Well, if both the husband and wife disagree, someone has to be in charge to make the final decision."

And again, I'll ask, "Why?"

After all, aren't both the husband and wife adults who are capable of making their own decisions and choices, and when they disagree, shouldn't they be able to find a way to reach a compromise? If two people who love each other enough to share their lives together can't accomplish that, what hope do we have?

I won't say that Mom and Dad always agreed on everything. They are both pretty strong-willed and independent. But I will say that I can't tell think of anything they disagreed on.

They worked it out, and stood together in the decisions they made. And that's another valuable lesson I've learned. Marriage shouldn't be a declaration of ownership; it should be an affirmation of affection and partnership.

It Seems to Me:
The Secret

We just celebrated my parents' sixty-first wedding anniversary. I say "we" because it was more than their celebration – it was our celebration of the example of love and commitment that they set for us. They give us all hope.

They make it look easy, but I know that they have had to face their fair share of challenges and trials. After all, life is like that. I grew up in their home, and I remember times when things seemed tough. Like most of us, financial concerns created stress for them, but they faced those issues together rather than letting them tear them apart.

Over the years, I've asked them for their secret, and each time I've gotten a different answer. It wasn't until recently that I realized their answers were meant to help me deal with my issues rather than explaining the secret of their successful marriage – and yet, perhaps each answer is a part of the whole.

Once Dad told me, "When you get married, you have to make that person the most important person in the world to you. Your friendships may still be important to you, but not as important as the person you marry. In fact, you should marry your best friend, and if you don't, you should make her your best friend. If you've picked the right person, she will do the same. If she doesn't, be patient and set the example."

The example he set was more important than the advice he gave. There was never any doubt in my mind that Mom was the most important person in Dad's life. I'm not saying that they never fought, but I noticed that when they did fight, they never attacked each other. It was always, "I don't like what you did" and never "You are a terrible person."

And while their affection for one another was personal and private, they didn't hide it from the world. When I was living in Oregon, they came for a visit. I only turned my back on them for a second, and when I looked up, they were walking along the beach holding hands! At that time, they had only been married for forty years, but it still took me by surprise.

In fact, just yesterday I caught them flirting with each other.

When asked for her advice on staying together, Mom said, "You find the person you love and just keep working on it."

Neither of them said, "When you meet the right person, everything just falls into place and becomes easy." It's not easy – it's just worth it.

"'Son' No other title worn with more pride."

Security

Kris Kristofferson's bitter
Wailing is enveloped
In grey mists.
"Don't send me no more
Goddam pain,"
He cries.
I stare at empty walls
That carry the stamp
Of my personality.
All signs of life here are
Artificial,
Like vows of love,
Words like forever,
Diet Coke,
And Dawnna.
Even tomorrow's pain is
Unreal
Next to
Yesterday's
Goodby.
"There is security
In numbness,"s
I think
As I send Jack Daniels
Chasing
A six-pack of Ranier.

Fall from Grace

For a Moment ...

I held the sun in my heart --
I felt Heaven touch my face.
For a Moment ...
I danced with Angels --
I heard the Music of Life,
And I sang with the Wind.

But now, my feet are back on the Ground.

My soul longs to soar --
My Heart cries for the sun --
My voice is lost
In the Stillness of the Night,
And I long to hold you once more ...

But, my feet are back on the Ground.

It Seems to Me:
Trust

*L*ately I've been reminded of the scene in the old Disney cartoon, *The Jungle Book,* where Mowgli is hypnotized by the python Kaa. "Trus-s-s-st me," Kaa whispers as he coils around Mowgli.

For me, that scene perfectly captures the way manipulative people use "trust" to get what they want. There is the salesperson who says, "A handshake should be enough for honest people!" (To which I have learned to respond, "And honest people are willing to back up their word with their signature on a piece of paper.") Of course, there are the politicians, some of whom sincerely make promises they can't back up while others simply lie.

And, of course, there are the honest salespeople and politicians who carry the stigma created by others. We start out with a healthy skepticism, and eventually they are able to win our trust.

At least with salespeople and politicians, we are usually prepared to deal with these trust issues. In a sense, we expect them.

It's a lot more complicated when it comes to personal relationships. A few days ago, one of my friends posted a comment on Face Book that said, "Love cannot exist without trust."

I responded with my own comment about how manipulative people will say things like, "If you loved me, you'd trust me," as if trust were something given automatically along with affection. "If you love me," I responded, "you'll understand that I've made the mistake of trusting the wrong people too soon, and you'll be willing to earn my trust."

I was a little surprised by the responses I got from people apologizing for having a hard time trusting others. They felt as though something was wrong with them because of their doubts and concerns.

Trust does not come automatically, and the more a person's trust has been abused, the more difficult it is to earn it. The blame doesn't belong on the shoulders of the victims; it belongs on the shoulders of the people who have abused their trust. Just as an honest salesperson should be willing to put their promises in writing, someone seeking another's trust should be willing to prove they deserve it. Any you should never feel guilty about wanting to protect yourself, especially when experience has taught you some painful lessons.

Just one more point – it is possible to feel affection toward someone in spite of the fact that you don't trust them. As a parent, there have been many times that I didn't trust my daughters. That doesn't mean that I thought they were bad kids, I just recognized the fact that they didn't always make the best choices. I never stopped loving them; I simply watched them closely until I was sure they had learned to make better choices.

And as a teacher, I try to start out trusting all of my students, but I have learned from experience that some students cheat, and so I have rules to help my students avoid even the appearance of cheating. On occasion, when I've asked students to remove their headphones during a test, I've had them complain that I didn't trust them. I respond by saying, "I don't know you well enough to trust you."

Perhaps we should use at least that much caution in our personal relationships.

"Trust does not come automatically."

Eating Fry-Bread with
Paula Gunn Allan

Her poems are tall, strong, sometimes fierce,
So I was surprised to see her
Small, round figure and the smile
That teetered on the brink of laughter.

We sat outside the Blue-Eyed Indian Bookstore,
Run by Leslie's mom,
Displaying Leslie's dad's photographs,
And we talked about Leslie
As we ate Indian Fry-Bread
And watched the sun set.

"This is good," Ken exclaims.
Paula winks at me and shakes her head.
Leave it to the educated white man
To feel a need to put words to the experience
Of having oven-hot fry-bread, melted butter,
Sweet berry jam swirl in the mouth until it becomes
Part of us, tasting history (the bread baked in earthen ovens
More than a thousand years old,
Fried in black White Man pans,

Jam made by berries picked and mixed by hands taught
By her mother,
Who was taught by her mother,
Who was taught ...).

And Ken calls it "good."
Paula and I look at the sun,
Watch as it spreads its crimson and orange fire
Across the horizon,
Mixing colors with the deep earth red of the desert
And the dark grey stone of the mesa.

"Yes," Paula says. "It's good."
For a moment, I understand the poet.

Love Is Only a Feeling

The old man was sleeping
When I climbed on board the bus.
I wanted time to think
So I took the seat next to him.
I had lost a lover
And felt only an emptiness.
The old man stirred
As the sunlight started to dim.
I was able to ignore him
Until he said,
"Excuse me, Son.
You seem awful quiet and troubled.
Maybe I can help.
It's none of my business,
What's happened or what you've done,
But I see from your eyes
That you've lost someone.
There are a couple of things
I'd like to say –
Things I wish I'd been told.
Never ask for more
Than what you already have,
And don't waste today wishing
For something you've already had.

We have no choice but to take
Whatever life has to give.
Whether we take it good
Or cry over the things we've lost
Makes the difference
In the lives we live.
So whether your life goes smoothly
Or you find yourself knocked around,
Enjoy what you have –
While you can.
And if you lose it,
Just move on.
Because, after all,
Love is only a feeling,
And forever is only a word."
Then the old man fell asleep.
I never saw him again
After I got off the bus,
But sometimes I wonder
If he really meant what he said
When he said
That love is only a feeling
And forever is only a word.

Dragon of Despair

"I believe in the darkness the
truth I saw in the light."
—Diane Makaeli

The Dragon of Despair
Strikes in the darkness,
Firing arrows of doubt
And insecurity,
Like an old foe,
Often defeated,
Yet returning to plague me
Once more.
Even the darkness
Is familiar,
I've been here before,
Lost in loneliness,
Searching for a flicker
Of hope
To light the way.
And I've survived,
And will survive again.
Only this time

I will win.
Carrying the burden
Of wounds from
Other battles --
Scars of loss
And disappointment --
I reach for
The sword of truth,
For in that truth
Shines the light of hope.
"What has been
Does not have to be,"
A soothing voice whispers.
"Hold on to truth,
For it lights the way
To tomorrow."
Last night,
The battle raged.

The Dragon was
Defeated
With the truth
I've seen
In your eyes.
I will face him
Again,
But for now,
The battle is won.

It Seems to Me:
Grief

Several years ago, my oldest daughter, Stevie Rae, lost a stuffed animal – Puppy Teddy – and I wrote a column about how much she grieved over it. I pointed out that, from an adult perspective, it might seem a little silly to be so upset over the loss of a toy, but from her perspective, she had lost her best friend and constant companion.

Stevie Rae is now an adult and the mother of two beautiful girls. What little hair I have left has grown grey, and I've had too many opportunities to learn more about grief. I've lost a sister, a few close friends, my grandparents, and an uncle. I've learned that the grief of having a relationship end can be as devastating as losing a loved one.

And it is even more difficult to watch someone you care for struggle with their grief. We hate to see them hurt, and we try to find ways to make them feel better. In doing so, we often say things that undermine their feelings and add to the burden they are carrying. Things like, "You've got to let it go" and "You've got to get over it," or the classic "Time heals all wounds" fail to recognize the fact that feelings of grief are valid and powerful.

Sometimes it's best to say nothing at all, but rather to listen with compassion and understanding. To let them know they are not alone in their grief. Just being there does make a difference.

We all grieve differently, and we shouldn't allow others to tell us how we should feel. We can't even choose that ourselves. Each of us must find our own path through the darkness; we have to allow ourselves to feel what we feel without guilt or embarrassment. As Melinda Smith and Jeanne Segal point out, "In order to heal, you have to acknowledge the pain." It is real, it is valid, and it is our own.

There are no time limits to grief. Maria V. Snyder wrote, "I do know it never disappears. An ember still smolders inside me. Most days, I don't notice it, but out of the blue, it'll flare to life." Perhaps grief never completely disappears – we just have to find a way to live with it.

And in a way, grief is an affirmation of our ability to love. After all, we wouldn't experience that feeling of loss if we didn't first care.

Two Short Poems

Beautiful Flower

Today I saw a beautiful flower,
Its soft purple blossom smiling at the sun,
And I thought,
"Go ahead and raise your proud face,
But be glad my love is not with me today.
For, next to her, your beauty is small,
And you would hide your face in shame."

Morning Haiku

For us, time floats like
Gossamer silk caressing
The petals of a perfect rose.

Simply Life

Rushing home on the freeway
(Which, at 5:00, means lunging five feet,
Stopping for a minute,
Then lunging another five feet)
My heart is filled with thoughts of you.
My day is so complex,
Dozens of choices,
None of them quite wrong (right?).
"Make a decision, then make it work."
On the radio, the talk is of relationships,
Or lack of them, In this complex world.
"It's all about sex," the speaker declares.
I listen because his logic is simple,
Not like the news that spewed from the radio
Before I changed the channel.
I don't agree, but I know I don't agree.
Because I have you.
You make my life simple.
I live to love you,
And I love you more each day.

It Seems to Me:
Picking Priorities

Sometimes I find myself talking to my students about success. Since I teach college level classes, it's a little surprising to learn that most of them have not thought much about long-term success. Their goals were pretty much set for them – finish high school, go to college, get a degree, and then get a job.

When I ask them to describe success, they describe symptoms of success – a nice house, a good family, a new car. Sometimes they will go so far as to mention "a good-paying job."

I'll suggest that, since they are preparing themselves for careers that they will take up thirty years of their lives or more, maybe they should be preparing themselves for futures they will enjoy living.

All too often, we present possibilities based entirely on practical considerations. This makes sense considering the cost and time involved in obtaining a college degree. But it gets a little scary when you look at certain realities.

The world of work is changing rapidly. Jobs that provided decent livings just a few years ago are no longer available, and many will find careers that don't even exist yet. Important jobs that were once considered honorable and worthy of respect are now viewed with derision.

So the young person who dreams of owning a farm or ranch sets off on a path that will leads away from the lifestyle that would bring them happiness. The one who really wants to be a teacher chooses to go into business management instead.

I'm not suggesting that it's wrong to be practical, but I am suggesting that there may be other things to consider. Teaching doesn't pay well, but it provides an opportunity to make a positive difference in people's lives. Ranching may be filled with uncertainty, but there's a lot to be said about living a life that is closely connected to nature and the land. Besides, we will always need food.

No matter what we choose to do with our lives, there will always be challenges and obstacles. When we make our choices based entirely on the likelihood of getting a job and earning good money, those obstacles appear overwhelming and we become easily discouraged.

But when we choose careers that spark a passion within us, we become more willing to face those challenges and overcome those obstacles. We may not be successful, but at least we fight for something we believe in.

The secret seems to be in picking our priorities. And each of us has to discover the things that matter most to us.

Another Quarter Begins

The mosaic of student faces, both young and old,
Fill the classrooms at Highline as another quarter begins.
A diverse community of humanity
Collected from across the globe
Gathered at the crossroads of
The Kent/Des Moines and Pacific Highway,
A few blocks from International Boulevard.
Hearts filled with life-changing dreams and desires,
They seek excellence
In the classrooms, in the college,
And within themselves.

It Seems to Me:
Why I (Attempt to) Teach

*I*t's a little surprising how often I'm asked why I became a teacher. Perhaps it's not the question itself that I find so surprising, but the way it's asked. Though it's usually unsaid, the tone of the question is closer to, "Of all the things you could have done with your life, what in the world made you want to be a teacher."

The answer that springs to my mind is usually, "I wanted to make a positive difference in people's lives," but like many things associated with teaching, that's too simple.

Perhaps I should start by explaining what I believe education is all about. In a way, it's funny because so many people talk about education without really understanding what it is. Actually, that's one of the tragedies of education today – everyone seems to be an expert, yet few people really understand what it is.

For many, the word "education" simply refers to the transfer of knowledge and information from one person or group of people to another. The tragedy behind this is that we then jump to the conclusion that we can measure the effectiveness of education by coming up with a standard test and find out how many facts have been transferred.

But education is more than that. If that were all there was

to it, the need for teachers would have been eliminated when the printing press was invented –indeed, many today feel that the need for teachers has been eliminated by the internet. Unfortunately (or fortunately, if you happen to be a teacher) that is far from the truth. Education is much, much more than simply imparting information.

The most important thing that education can accomplish is to teach students how to learn. We live in a world that is constantly changing – the "truths" that we readily accepted yesterday are being challenged today. Today's highest paying jobs didn't exist twenty years ago, and the jobs that our students will hold haven't been created yet. We don't just teach our students "stuff," but we have to teach them how to wade through mountains of misinformation in order to find the truth, and then we have to teach them how to understand that truth.

This is especially difficult in a world where we are constantly confronted with the idea that there are only two ways to see things – the right way and the wrong way. In our hearts, we may recognize that is too simplistic, that the world is much more complex. Yet, we get caught up in countless battles where proving that our point of view is right, an anything different is not only wrong, but it's evil and will destroy us.

So, why do I teach? I want to make a positive difference in the lives of my students. I want to help them see the complexities of life and be prepared to deal with them. I don't want to teach them what to think – I want to help them learn how to think. I want them to be prepared for the changes they will face throughout their lives so that they will face their futures with curiosity – not fear.

Casual Conversation

Today I thought I'd say,
"You are beautiful."
And "I get lost
When I look into your eyes."
Then I would gently brush your hair
From your face,
Feel your soft, smooth cheek,
The warmth of your smile.
You would move closer to me,
Lightly touch my arm.
Our lips would meet,
We would hold each other close,
Feel the rhythm of our hearts beat as one.
I thought I'd say,
"You are beautiful,
I think of you all the time.
The sound of your voice is a song
I carry in my heart.
Your sweet, natural scent
Makes me feel alive,
Giddy,
Young--
Like a colt, anxious to run across the desert.

I want to bury my face in your hair,
Taste the salty sweetness of your throat,
Lose myself in your love."
I thought I'd say you are beautiful--
But I didn't.
I just said,
"Hi. How's it going?"
Casual conversation.
Nothing inappropriate.
No threat.
No risk.
Nothing lost.
Nothing gained.
But I did get lost in your eyes.

Best Friend

I want to be the man I see
When I look into your eyes.
The man who's courage rules his life
Whose dreams fill the skies.
The poet not afraid to love,
Who believes true love never dies.
I want to learn about you.
When I look into your eyes.
What you think.
How you feel.
What your dreams are
How I can help make them real.
I want to tell you
Your smile warms my soul -- helps it heal.
That your voice
Is the song of my heart.
When we're apart,
I doubt you will ever feel this way for me.
But when we're together
I see in your eyes
The man I've always wanted to be.

Poppa's Sonnet

The day begins with gentle taps upon
The door of my solitary abode.
I rush to catch the little scamp who's gone
Around the corner like a little toad.
"Rannen! Rannen!" I call, then wait to hear
The gentle music of her gay reply.
It's quiet: she is hiding somewhere near.
At last! "Poppa! Poppa!" I hear her cry.
She carries sunshine, song, and love
Into each room she graces with her dance.
And though I'm old I just can't get enough
Of my granddaughter's joyful, sweet presence.
My little scamp, the daughter of my daughter.
My light, my joy, my beautiful granddaughter.

To My Best Friend

"The story of your life has not been
written yet. You're still writing it."
—Maya Angelou

Who would have imagined
When our story began
That we would someday find
Ourselves here?
It's hard to see beyond the beauty;
Turquoise eyes,
A smile that lifts heavy hearts,
The soft, gentle face that steals my breath
And holds it hostage until I am dizzy;
But the strength of your spirit,
Facing challenges, overcoming obstacles;
Your generous heart that sees the need in others
And shows them the treasures within their souls;
A mind that sees the sense of things
That remain a mystery to me;
These are the true treasures hidden beneath
The beauty that others can see.

It's no surprise that we
Became best friends,
And continue growing closer.
And now, I find myself
Wanting to skip to the next chapter
In the story of our lives
To see what the future might be.
But the story is written
One day at a time,
So I will wait
Almost patiently
To learn the answer
To this mystery.

It Seems to Me:
An Act of Courage

When we think of heroes, we usually think of dramatic scenes that are larger-than-life, and some of the most heroic acts slip by without notice.

Last week I witnessed an act of courage that reminded me of the great examples that have been and continue to be set for me.

A few months ago, my best friend, Diane, was injured in a riding accident. She was told that she should never get on a horse again, but she wouldn't accept that. She loves horses, and being able to ride is an important part of who she is.

Last week I was able to be there when Diane faced her fears and climbed back into the saddle.

And she did have to overcome her fears. She didn't want to be hurt again. She was afraid that she would climb into the saddle and discover that she had lost that special connection she's always had with horses. She had family and friends who tried to talk her out of doing it.

But she also realized that she would not be true to herself if she let her fears stand in her way.

We all face challenges in our lives. Too many times, we allow our fears to keep us from being true to ourselves. We stay in unhealthy relationships because we are afraid of being alone, or we avoid relationships because we are afraid of being hurt. We work at jobs that make us miserable because we are afraid of being unemployed, and we veer away from the career paths we desire because we are afraid we'll fail.

Too many times, when we do decide it's time to meet our challenges head-on, the people we expect to encourage and support us become obstacles. For whatever reason -- concern for our well-being or fear that we may accomplish something that they didn't have the courage to try, they seek to discourage us. A good friend, Ed Fine, recently told me, "When we make a decision with determination, it's amazing what we can accomplish."

But it takes determination and courage, and most of us fall short of our dreams because we are afraid to try.

And then, every once in awhile, someone like Diane reminds us that, with courage and determination, we can overcome our fears and rescue our true selves.

Spirit of the Horse

An eagle flew overhead today
Carrying its message
From the earth --
Calling my spirit to soar.
The land calls,
Beckoning us to ride free
Among the dusty foothills
Of the Rockies,
Turquoise blue skies overhead,
Craggy peaks at my back,
And you by my side.
The earth speaks through
The Spirit of the Horse,
Hooves beating the rhythm
Of our souls.
An eagle flies overhead,
But all becomes clear
On the back of a horse
Whose spirit connects mine
To the earth,
To the sky,
And to the woman I love.

"The earth speaks through the Spirit of the Horse ..."

Diane's Eyes

Sometimes,
In the Rocky Mountain valley
I call home,
Afternoon rainstorms
Gently caress the western peaks
While the skies overhead
Are clear
And as blue as a calm Pacific sea.
As the sun sets, it paints the rain
Fiery red
Against the canvas
Of deep purple clouds,
And it's the most
Beautiful thing
I had ever seen --
Until I looked into your eyes.

Beautiful Cowgirl

Your smile touches my heart,
And I yearn to hold you near me again.
There may be miles between us,
Yet our souls reach across the distance
To embrace one another each day.
My best friend, my Cowgirl –
The Princess of my Heart.
Beautiful words, beautiful names,
Music to my ears.
How I long to hear the music of your voice,
To taste the sweetness of your lips,
To feel your warmth beside me.
My best friend, my Cowgirl –
The Princess of my Heart.
You are the music in my song,
The light in my life,
My joy!

"There may be miles between us, Yet our souls reach across the distance ..."

The Promise

I know I can't chase away the pain,
But I'll always be at your side
When you cry.

And I can't promise the sun
Will always shine,
But I'll take your hand
And walk with you
Through the Rain.

I'll be the light
In your darkness,
As you are in mine.

I'll hold you up
When you need
Someone to lean on.

And when you feel
Doubt or fear,
My love will always be there
For you to hold on to.

"I'll be the light In your darkness, As you are in mine ..."